THE OLDEST IRISH TRADITION: A WINDOW ON THE IRON AGE

THE OLDEST IRISH TRADITION: A WINDOW ON THE IRON AGE

BY

KENNETH
HURLSTONE JACKSON
F.B.A.

Professor of Celtic,
Edinburgh University

THE REDE LECTURE
1964

CAMBRIDGE
AT THE UNIVERSITY PRESS
1964

PUBLISHED BY
THE SYNDICS OF THE CAMBRIDGE UNIVERSITY PRESS

Bentley House, 200 Euston Road, London, N.W. 1
American Branch: 32 East 57th Street, New York 22, N.Y.
West African Office: P.O. Box 33, Ibadan, Nigeria

CAMBRIDGE UNIVERSITY PRESS

1964

Printed in Great Britain at the University Printing House, Cambridge
(Brooke Crutchley, University Printer)

To my parents

ABBREVIATIONS

BG   Caesar, *De Bello Gallico*.

CEP   M. Tierney, 'The Celtic Ethnography of Poseidonius', *PRIA*, LX (1959–60), c.

CS   T. P. Cross and C. H. Slover, *Ancient Irish Tales* (New York, Holt, 1936).

GL   H. M. and N. K. Chadwick, *The Growth of Literature*, I (Cambridge, 1932).

PBA   *Proceedings of the British Academy*.

PRIA   *Proceedings of the Royal Irish Academy*.

SMMD   R. Thurneysen, *Scéla Mucce Meic Dathó* (Mediaeval and Modern Irish Series, vol. VI; Dublin, 1935).

TBC I   Version I of the Cattle Raid of Cooley, edited by J. Strachan and J. G. O'Keefe, *The Táin Bó Cúailnge* (Dublin, 1912).

TBC II   Version II of the Cattle Raid of Cooley, edited by E. Windisch, *Die Altirische Heldensage Táin Bó Cúalnge* (Leipzig, 1905).

ZCP   *Zeitschrift für Celtische Philologie*.

MEDIEVAL IRISH literary tradition contains material of very great diversity. There are lyric and panegyric poems, historical and pseudo-historical and antiquarian texts, stories of pure entertainment, a great deal of religious matter, and much else. The pseudo-historical literature includes tales about what it alleges were the various immigrant races who invaded and inhabited Ireland in ancient times, treated on the surface as if they were genuine historical peoples. Just below the surface, however, some of them if not all appear to exhibit the marks of pagan gods or other supernatural beings, and are therefore more or less comparable to the 'myths' of Greek literature. But as soon as one tries to fish for this mythology from under the surface much of it slips through one's net, leaving for the most part little but the names of characters unquestionably recognisable, from their Romano-Gaulish and Romano-British counterparts, or less certainly from some features of the stories about them, as having been Celtic gods at an earlier stage. About the religious beliefs connected with them we are largely ignorant, and of the manner of their worship completely so. Besides, it is evident that the medieval Irish antiquarians who made these things into 'histories' were almost as ignorant of such points as we are, though needless to say their works have been a gold-mine for the speculations of scholars.

Side by side with these and various other classes of literary material there is another, and quite different, body of narrative in the very early Irish tradition; one which belongs to the genre of literature of entertainment and contains very little that can reasonably or safely be taken for myth, or ought to be interpreted as such. This is a group of prose tales purporting to describe a 'heroic' stage in Ireland's distant past, telling of the wars and adventures of a group of characters thought of as having been real people, living long ago in a setting which it is implied was a genuine one. To anticipate, the situation is very like that of the heroes of the *Iliad*, and like the *Iliad* the stories are told on the whole with straightforward realism as if they had really happened, though without any specific implication that this is history. This realism is nevertheless broken by at least two non-realistic elements. First, some few of the characters are clearly supernatural and some of the scenes involve supernatural events and motifs. But here we are on familiar ground in the comparison with Homer, of course *mutatis mutandis*, since his gods and semi-divine beings, and the episodes in which they take part, are equally of a supernatural kind. Second, the realism is often

2

apt to be submerged in a burst of exaggeration, in deliberate fantasy, such as must have delighted the imagination of the early Irish audience but which is too often tedious and absurd to us, delaying and spoiling the straightforward vividness of the action. If we discount this side of the narrative, however, these stories are strikingly like the epics of other early literatures, as has often been pointed out; not only Homer but also *Beowulf*, the early German heroic poetry, and the rest. Indeed, except for the fact that the telling is mainly in prose—and this is really a detail—this whole body of tales *is* epic and ought to be discussed on the same footing, though too often it is ignored by students of epic literature. It is one of the many virtues of the work of the Chadwicks on early comparative literature that they have done full justice to this.

These epic tales, as they may be called, are relatively early even in their present dress; but the theme of this lecture is that in some form or other they have come down to us from a period which is a good deal earlier than that. It is not suggested for a moment that any of the people who act in them or any of the events described are historical, and indeed some of them are much too unreal for this to be possible. In any case there is no outside source which could corroborate the existence of any of the characters such as there is in the case of the German epics, with their Attila and Gunther and the others confirmed by the evidence of Greek and Latin authorities. What I do maintain is that the immediate setting of the oldest Irish hero tales, that is to say the state of endemic warfare between Ulster and the rest of Ireland, and various other features of the Irish political construction, material civilisation, and way of life, which are very archaic in appearance, very circumstantial, and on the whole very consistent, belong to a period some centuries earlier than the time when they were first written down—belong in fact to a '*pre*-historic' Ireland. There is nothing in such a hypothesis which need alarm us. After all, it is commonly believed that the immediate setting of the *Iliad*, the warlike expedition by the states of Mycenaean Greece against a city of Asia Minor, is very probably more or less genuine; that the cultural and political background, or at least a stratum or strata within that background, really does illustrate the conditions and way of life of the Mycenaean and sub-Mycenaean civilisation of the fourteenth–twelfth centuries B.C.; and that Homer in the eighth century was adapting material of which part had come down to him from that time. Up to a point, the political geography and various features in the material culture of the *Iliad* do not suit early historical Greece and do strikingly suit what we now know about 'pre-historic' Greece at the period in question. And this is all that is claimed for Ireland in this lecture. There is not in fact anything new in this—it is familiar to Celtic scholars and seems to be generally accepted by them; but Celtic scholars are unfortunately few, and historians, archaeologists, and others interested in the early history of the British Isles are I think much less aware of this extraordinary archaic fragment of European literature, and it is to them that this lecture is directed.

We know that the latest archaeological expression of the pre-Roman European Iron Age, the so-called La Tène culture, lasted in a vestigial form in Ireland, where there was no Roman occupation to swamp it, until at least the time when the introduction of Christianity in the fifth century brought with it considerable changes in intellectual and to some degree social organisation and particularly in art styles and motifs. I shall attempt to show that the background of the Irish epic tales appears to be older than these changes, and hence that when all due allowance is made for later accretions the stories provide us with a picture—very dim and fragmentary, no doubt, but still a picture—of Ireland in the Early Iron Age. If this strikes anyone present as an excessive claim, perhaps an unquestionable instance of a feature belonging to the Iron Age which can be proved to have survived into the Irish early Christian culture may help to make out a prima facie case. I refer to the motifs called collectively the 'trumpet pattern' which are so characteristic of the decorative style of the pre-

Roman Celtic Iron Age. These beautiful flowing curves, whose origins can be traced back to the fifth century B.C., typify La Tène art, particularly in the British Isles, as long as it lasted. Now, what replaced the La Tène art styles in Ireland was what is called 'early Christian' art, chiefly of Mediterranean origin, with its highly elaborate interlacing strap-work, chequer patterns, vine-scrolls, animals and birds of eastern textile inspiration, and Byzantine-looking human figures, which fused with other motifs into the 'Hiberno-Saxon' art of the seventh and later centuries as we see it in the great manuscripts like the Books of Durrow, Lindisfarne, and Kells and the early Christian metal-work and sculpture. Yet in almost any of the fully illuminated pages of Kells, and markedly also in Durrow, to quote only these, one finds panels partly decorated with unquestionable La Tène trumpet-pattern designs. The motif must have passed in Ireland from pre-Christian to Christian art at a single leap in its full vigour; and this is not really surprising when we remember that in Ireland there were no intervening centuries of Roman civilisation to destroy it and the La Tène culture to which it belonged. If so, it is surely also not so surprising that some of the *literary* traditions belonging to the Iron Age in Ireland should have lasted long enough to be adopted into the written literature of this very same early Christian period, once the use of writing became applied to the recording of the native literature. I shall hope to show that this is what did happen, and how it happened.

The body of heroic narrative in question is called the Ulster Cycle because it centres round the king of Ulster and his warriors. The greatest tale, and by far the longest, is the famous Cattle Raid of Cooley,[1] which tells of an expedition from Connaught to carry off a celebrated bull from Cooley near Dundalk on the borders of Ulster. Some of the others are the Story of Mac Dathó's Pig,[2] the Feast of Bricriu,[3] the Drunkenness of the Ulstermen,[4] and above all the classic tragedy of Deirdriu and the Exile of the Sons of Uisliu.[5] The Ulster of these stories is a great and powerful kingdom—*Ulaid*, 'the men of Ulster'—able to take on the rest of Ireland in war, the enemy being constantly referred to as *fir Érenn*, 'the men of Ireland'. Their capital fortress, the Irish Mycenae, was Emain Macha, now Navan Rath, a ruined hill-fort near Armagh. Their

[1] 'Version I' = *TBC* I; 'Version II' = *TBC* II. The first translated by Winifred Faraday, *The Cattle Raid of Cualnge* (Grimm Library, no. 16; London, 1904). The second translated into German by Windisch, *TBC* II, and into English by Joseph Dunn, *The Ancient Epic Tale Táin Bó Cúalnge* (London, 1914).

[2] Edition, see *SMMD*. Translation, *CS*, pp. 199 ff.

[3] Edited and translated by G. Henderson, *Fled Bricrend, the Feast of Bricriu* (London, Irish Texts Society, vol. II; 1899).

[4] Edited by J. C. Watson, *Mesca Ulad*, Mediaeval and Modern Irish Series, vol. XIII (Dublin, 1941); translated *CS*, pp. 215 ff.

[5] Edited and translated by V. Hull, *Longes Mac n-Uislenn* (New York, 1949); translated *CS*, pp. 239 ff.

over-king, the Agamemnon, is Conchobar, and under him is a group of aristocratic warriors like Homer's Achaeans; Cú Chulainn, the young heroic champion, the Achilles; Fergus, the wise old warrior, the Nestor; and so on. On the other side, the confederacy of 'the men of Ireland' is led by the king of Connaught, Ailill, and his strong-minded Amazon wife Medb, whose name means 'She who makes men drunk' or 'The Drunken Woman'. With these are their seven sons all called Maine, but distinguished by nicknames, and their daughter Findabair whose hand in marriage is used several times as a bribe; also various heroes from Connaught and elsewhere and the kings and armies of the rest of Ireland. These are the Trojans of the Irish epic, and their Troy is Cruachain, now the ruins of Rathcroghan in Co. Roscommon.

These stories constitute a classic case of what the Chadwicks defined as a *heroic* society.[1] The principle of it is a primitive aristocracy, a warrior aristocracy in the sense that it is organised for the warfare which is its business. Economically speaking it is chiefly a cattle-rearing community in Ireland, and cattle are the staple form of wealth and the aim of much of the raiding and fighting. We learn more about the structure of the earliest traceable Irish society from the Law tracts, which themselves contain a very ancient stratum and represent a very archaic state of

[1] See *GL*, chapter 4.

affairs.[1] Here the king comes at the top of the aristocratic pyramid, his chief nobles immediately below, the inferior nobles below that, and then the non-noble freemen who are primarily a landowning class but include also superior craftsmen; notably the blacksmith, who as maker of weapons, and perhaps reputed to have supernatural powers, was a person of real importance in this structure. Below this came the unfree, men who had no franchise and no right to bear arms; property-less men, tenant farmers, labourers, inferior craftsmen, and so on. Among freemen the relation of the vassal or client and his lord, which was a voluntary association terminable by agreement, was a fundamental institution. The vassal borrowed capital from the lord and repaid it with interest; he also gave him military service and attended and supported him as part of his retinue on public occasions. In return, the lord looked after the vassal's interests, particularly his interests at law, and protected him in time of trouble. It was the possession of vassals which gave the lord the rank of noble and so distinguished him from other freemen; moreover it gave him considerable influence, the greater as the number of his vassals was greater. The whole relation, with its reciprocal advantages and duties, reminds one of that

[1] For a full discussion of the structure of early Irish society see E. MacNeill, *Early Irish Laws and Institutions* (Dublin, n.d.; London, 1935).

9

between a Highland chief and his principal clansmen before 1745. The word for 'vassal' in early Irish is *céile* which means literally 'companion', no doubt used because of his important duty of taking part in the lord's retinue. So much is seen in the Laws; in the Ulster tales the institution is occasionally mentioned by name, as for instance where the Connaught messenger Mac Roth asks Cú Chulainn's charioteer whose *céile* he is, and he replies '*Céile* to that man yonder', pointing to Cú Chulainn, and when Mac Roth goes to him and asks him whose *céile* he is, the answer is '*Céile* to Conchobar', that is, to the king.[1]

A further aspect of the connection between lord and client is seen in the institution of fosterage. It was the practice that the young sons of an inferior noble were sent to live in the household of the superior, or in that of the king, to be brought up there and trained in the arts of war and the other duties of an aristocrat; which meant in effect that the inferior had given hostages to his chief. This established a bond between foster-father and foster-son, and particularly between foster-brothers, which was very close and sacred. The most truly tragic aspect of the tragic story of how Fer Diad was obliged to challenge Cú Chulainn and Cú Chulainn was obliged to fight and kill him is the fact that they were foster-brothers, and consequently the act was

[1] *TBC* I, ll. 1115 ff.

fratricide and an abomination. Here the terrible conflict between two duties is of the same kind as those we know in Greek tragedy.

Like much else in early Irish narrative, the Ulster tales show us that another key social group was the druids, who are actually called by this ancient Celtic name, plural *druid*. They were of course priests, but the part they play in the stories is that of prophets and soothsayers, since in the absence of passages about organised religion there is no scope for their priestly functions to appear. The chief druid of Ulster, Cathbad, is a familiar and important figure in the tales. Favourite servants seem to have had a somewhat privileged position, at any rate by custom, if we can judge from the relation between Cú Chulainn and his charioteer, who was in any case a freeman.

The Ulster tales concern themselves almost exclusively with the free class, and the unfree are scarcely even mentioned apart from an occasional reference to them as a rabble, apparently mainly thought of as camp followers. In this, of course, the stories agree closely with Homer and the rest. Since they deal with the aristocracy it is natural that the ideas and ideals are in fact those of a simple aristocratic warrior class, again as in Homer. The hero is above all greedy for fame. When the young Cú Chulainn discovers that he has unwittingly taken a step which makes it his fate that his life shall be short but his name shall be famous among the men of Ireland for deeds of valour, his only comment is, 'Provided that I shall be famous I do not care if I last in this world for only a single day'.[1] The coincidence with Achilles is striking. Achilles knows that he has the choice of staying at Troy to fight and being killed, but earning undying glory, or of deserting his comrades there and living a long life, but losing his fame; and as any hero would, he chooses the first.[2] So too Beowulf says, 'Let him who may, win himself fame before death, for that is best for a warrior in after times when he lives no more'. The Irish heroes are extremely touchy on points of honour, and bound to avenge any sort of insult with the greatest savagery; hence for instance Conchobar's implacable hatred of the sons of Uisliu for the abduction of his intended mistress Deirdriu, and the treacherous revenge he took on them in the sequel. The hero must always prove his superiority in fight—must 'always excel and be better than the rest',[3] in Homer's words—and a favourite way of doing this was by challenging the warriors of the opposite side to single combat. There are numerous examples of this in the Cattle Raid of Cooley, with Cú Chulainn always coming off best. Courage and fierceness are of course essential to the hero, and they are two of the primary aristocratic virtues. In this

---

[1] *TBC* I, ll. 571 f.   [2] *Iliad*, IX, 410 ff.
[3] *Iliad*, VI, 208.

connection I will mention now, and take up later, the promise which Conchobar's bodyguard make him before the final battle of the Cattle Raid: '"We will stand our ground," said the warriors, "though the earth should split under us and the sky above on us."'[1]

Side by side with all this, however, there is a rough sense of decency and fair play—it is not honourable to take advantage of a helpless enemy, because it is not worthy of a hero. For instance there is a striking scene in the Cattle Raid of Cooley[2] where Cú Chulainn comes upon a Connaught charioteer who is cutting wood to replace a broken chariot-pole. The man does not know him, and, taking him for one of his own people, asks his help in stripping the bark and twigs from the poles he has cut. Presently he discovers who his fellow-worker is, and gives himself up for lost, but Cú Chulainn tells him not to be afraid, for he never kills charioteers. Here the coincidence is remarkable with the scene in the *Iliad* where Achilles catches one of the sons of Priam cutting wood for a chariot rail, but the sequel is different, for the Trojan is an armed warrior, not an unarmed servant beneath the notice of a hero, and Achilles therefore kills him.[3] Indeed, Cú Chulainn sometimes pushes his sense of fair play to extremes, as he does in the episode where a

---

[1] *TBC* I, ll. 3576 ff.   [2] *TBC*, I, ll. 770 ff.
[3] *Iliad*, XXI, 34 ff.

13

Connaught warrior called Etarcomal tries to goad him to fight. Etarcomal thinks Cú Chulainn is an inexperienced and boastful boy, but Cú Chulainn knows very well that he can easily dispose of Etarcomal, and with surprising magnanimity, he treats his rude taunts with patience, refusing to be provoked. Obviously he feels that to be irritated to fighting such a fool would be like stealing pennies from a blind man; once again, an unworthy act. Finally, however, after some pretty convincing if more or less harmless practical warnings of his superiority, such as shaving off his hair with one stroke of the sword without scratching his scalp, Cú Chulainn is obliged to kill Etarcomal, which he does by almost splitting him in two halves.[1] So again, Cú Chulainn finds unprotected no less a person than the queen of Connaught herself, the cause of all the trouble for Ulster. 'Spare me', says Medb. 'If I did kill you I should be quite justified', says Cú Chulainn, but he lets her go unhurt because he used not to kill women.[2] Something like all this is seen in Achilles' treatment of Priam when he comes to ransom the body of Hector, though of course that scene is far greater because of Homer's immense poetic superiority. Along with all this, another aspect of the heroic mind is the generosity which was demanded of the hero. This too was an aristocratic virtue—it was unworthy of a noble to

[1] *TBC* i, ll. 1175 ff.   [2] *TBC* i, ll. 3640 ff.

14

be mean, and extravagant liberality in giving gifts was expected. In general the ideals and habits of this society are of a rather adolescent nature, but the high sense of tragedy and drama to which the narrative may sometimes rise may lift it to great heights, much as the rather childish quarrel of Achilles with Agamemnon motivates one of the greatest poems of all literature.

A good deal is to be learned from the Irish tales about the clothing, weapons, houses, and other aspects of what is called the material culture of these people. The men wore a long woollen mantle pinned at the neck with a brooch of silver or of gold decorated with engraving or gems; and underneath, a tunic reaching to the knee. The cloth is sometimes described as woven or embroidered with gold thread. It is doubtful whether trousers are clearly mentioned in the earliest sources. The women also wore mantles, and tunics to the feet, and did their hair in two or three plaits fastened with decorated beads. For weapons the warrior carried one or two throwing javelins or a broad-bladed thrusting spear, and a long iron sword, often described as gold-hilted, which accounts of fighting show was used as a sabre for cutting rather than as a rapier for thrusting. Another common weapon was the sling, and Cú Chulainn was particularly skilful in the use of this. He himself possessed a horrible spear called the *gae bulga*, a phrase of uncertain meaning. The whole question of this spear is surrounded with doubts of various kinds,[1] but it does seem to have been thought of as so hideously barbed that it could not be extracted, and a wound with it was bound to be deadly.[2] So too Cú Chulainn's divine father Lug is described as carrying a five-pointed spear and a forked javelin,[3] and five-pointed spears are mentioned elsewhere.[4] There is no mention anywhere in the early texts of the use of bows and arrows, though they occur in later sources; and it is significant that even the names for these, once they do appear, are foreign loan-words, respectively *boga* from the Norse *bógi* and *saiget* from the Latin *sagitta*, the former of which can scarcely have been borrowed before the ninth century. It would seem that the warriors of the Ulster tales were not acquainted with the bow and arrow. The only defensive armour which is at all clearly envisaged is the shield, made of alder wood, apparently round, and with a decorated metal rim. The most characteristic equipment of the ancient Irish warrior must have been the spear and shield, for the word *gaisced*, the set of weapons formally presented to a youth on

[1] I am well aware, for instance, that it has been held to be a purely mythological object, standing for a lightning flash (see T. F. O'Rahilly, *Early Irish History and Mythology*, Dublin, 1946, pp. 61 ff.); as well as of other explanations. But this sort of thing, particularly considering the arguments offered in support, is not one with which I find myself in much sympathy.

[2] Cf. *TBC* I, l. 2690.   [3] *TBC* I, l. 1795.

[4] E.g. *TBC* I, l. 3187.

16

reaching manhood, is an old compound meaning originally 'spear and shield', and *gaiscedach*, 'a warrior', was 'one bearing a spear and shield'. Unfortunately, the meanings of some of the words describing dress, weapons, and the like are by no means clear, and the accounts of them, though vivid, are nevertheless often tantalisingly vague, so that an attempt to equate them with what we know from archaeological or other sources is not always to be trusted.[1] A careful collection and analysis of all these terms is very badly needed before further progress can be made along these lines.[2]

The really notable feature about battle tactics is the use of the war-chariot. To judge from descriptions as well as probabilities these were very light and strong. They were drawn by two horses yoked to a pole, and had two wheels with iron tyres and a seat on which the warrior sat. The chariot was manœuvred by a charioteer using a goad, and the tactic seems to have been that he drove the chariot at the enemy and the warrior himself hurled his spears at them. The Irish heroes are called by the

[1] Thus the Irish *delg nduillech*, 'leafy brooch', identified by Ridgeway with the La Tène 'leaf brooch' (*PBA*, II, 24), may easily have been something quite different; not to mention the fact that the object is apparently spoken of in relatively late texts only.

[2] A beginning was made by Bauersfeld in *ZCP*, XIX, 294 ff., but he deals almost exclusively with weapons, and only with some of them.

term *eirr* which means 'chariot man', as if the possession of a chariot was their main characteristic, very much as the medieval term *eques*, 'knight', is strictly speaking 'horseman, a soldier who fights on horseback'. The chariot horses were the hero's favourite animals and the charioteer his favoured servant and familiar counsellor. Cú Chulainn's chariot, which of course had to be more wonderful than anyone else's, is described as being armed with spikes and hooks and blades, to cut down any infantry who got in its way, but this is part of a late, interpolated passage in the Cattle Raid of Cooley,[1] and it is therefore uncertain whether it represents anything early.

When a young man reached manhood he seems to have been ceremonially initiated into the status of a warrior by receiving from his lord a set of weapons, a spear and shield, precisely the *gaisced* just mentioned, and formally mounted a chariot. This ceremony was called 'taking arms', and it bears a loose resemblance to that associated with receiving knighthood in medieval Europe. It was thereupon his duty to gather his men and lead them on a raid against the nearest hostile district, returning if possible with spoils of cattle. This is specifically called an Ulster practice in the Story of Mac Dathó's Pig, where Cet, one of the Connaught heroes, says, 'It is a custom among you Ulstermen

[1] *TBC* I, ll. 1964 ff.

18

that every youth who takes arms among you makes us the goal of his hockey-playing'.[1] A further custom very characteristic of the Irish hero tales is the habit rather loosely called 'head-hunting'. When a warrior killed an enemy he might cut off his head and bring it away with him as a trophy. In the tale just mentioned the same Cet is challenged by the Ulster hero Conall Cernach, who says, 'Since I took spear in my hand I have not been without killing a Connaught man every single day, and without destructive fire every single night, and I have never slept without the head of a Connaught man under my knee'. Cet confesses that Conall is the better warrior, and wishes his brother were present, as he would have been a match for Conall. 'He *is* present, however', says Conall, and brings out his head and hurls it at Cet.[2] It was prophesied of this Conall at his birth that he would be a great enemy of Connaught and hunter of their heads,[3] and he certainly appears in this role in the hero tales. The displaying of heads as trophies is seen for instance in the story of how Conall avenged Cú Chulainn's death, bringing the heads of those who had killed him, showing them to his widow, and telling how he himself had won them. A different aspect of the same idea is found in the text called The Death of

[1] *SMMD*, § 9. [2] *SMMD*, § 16.

[3] *Cóir Anmann*, § 251 (W. Stokes and E. Windisch, *Irische Texte*, III, ii, 392 f.).

Conchobar. Conall had killed a Connaught man called Meis Gegra, took out his brains, and mixed them with lime so that they made a hard ball, and kept this on a shelf, but Cet stole the ball and used it as a sling-stone with which he wounded Conchobar. The tale begins with Conall calling for the brain-ball to show it off to the Ulstermen as a trophy, and the narrator comments on this Ulster custom, saying that when they were boasting of their deeds in competition with one another, comparing their trophies, it was the practice of the Ulstermen to send for these brain-balls to display them.[1]

A favourite setting for a story is at a feast in the hall of a chief. The hall seems to have been a fairly large building, made of a wooden frame with weather-boarding, and roofed with shingles; inside, the roof was held up by carved and decorated pillars. There was a fire on the floor and a vent in the roof for the smoke. All round the walls, apparently between the pillars, was a range of what one might call compartments, like a row of boxes at a theatre, raised somewhat above the level of the floor and perhaps separated from one another by partitions or curtains. In these 'boxes', called *imdai*, the chief heroes sat at the feast, each in his own *imdae* with his immediate followers about him; and thence he could look out into the body of the hall and watch

[1] K. Meyer, *Death Tales of the Ulster Heroes* (Royal Irish Academy Todd Lecture Series, XIV; 1906), p. 4.

his fellow-guests. Very likely they slept there too when the feast was over. On the level of an upper floor there seems to have been a sort of balcony projecting outwards, called *grianán*, 'a sunny place', where the women could sit and sew and look out over the countryside beyond the fortifications. There would be other associated buildings, and the whole was surrounded by a defensive rampart with a parapet walk and stockade, a great gate, and a porter's lodge; and outside that there was a cleared space like a parade-ground.

The food served at feasts was chiefly meat; beef, veal, and above all pork, which was clearly the favourite food. Whole roast pigs were carved, and there was meat in cauldrons into which one thrust a flesh-fork to bring out a lump. Cakes of flour baked with honey are mentioned. Vats full of wine, beer, and mead were provided, and servants carried round food and drink. It was the right of the best hero present to carve the chief carcass for the diners, and this was a practical as well as a symbolic privilege, since the carver was expected to give himself the best joint of the meat, the *curadmír* or 'Champion's Portion'. This was indeed the bone of contention, and it is the theme of stories built up round this claim—for who *was* the best hero present? Naturally several warriors might demand the privilege, and to make this good each abused the other, quoting discreditable stories about past disgraces which had befallen his rival or his rival's relatives; whereupon the other might sit down to hide his blushes. In the Story of Mac Dathó's Pig, the Connaught hero Cet puts a whole series of Ulstermen to shame in this way and wins the right to the Champion's Portion. A typical passage is as follows: "'More contest!' said Cet. "You shall have it," said Cuscraid the Stammerer, son of Conchobar. "Who's this?" said Cet. "Cuscraid," said everyone. "He looks like a king's heir."[1] "No thanks to you," said the youth. "Good," said Cet; "it was to us that you first came when you first took arms. We met on the borderland. You left behind a third of your people, and went off with a spear through your neck, so that you cannot produce a word properly for yourself, for the spear destroyed the sinews of your neck, and you have been called Cuscraid the Stammerer ever since." He put the whole province to shame in this way.'[2] Sometimes, though, the opponent would not be put down with words, and then they came to blows, and the right to the Champion's Portion might then only be gained by one killing the other. The heroes hung up their weapons on the wall when they sat down to a feast, but they were evidently not uncomfortably

[1] This sentence is generally taken as part of what 'everyone' said, but the context seems rather to imply that it was said by Cet, as an unwilling compliment.

[2] SMMD, § 14.

far away. Apart from feasting, other popular pastimes were hunting, listening to the poems, music, and tales of the entertainers, and some sort of board-game called *fidchell*. This is commonly translated 'chess' for lack of a better term, but it cannot really have been chess; if we may judge from the tenth-century board discovered at Ballinderry crannog in Co. Westmeath it was one in which the two sets of 'men' were pegged into fixed positions on the board. The youths also played a team-game called *báire*, with clubs and balls, the object being to score by hitting the ball into the opposing team's goal, a hole in the ground. It was thus more or less an early form of hockey or similar games.

The druids already mentioned commonly appear in the hero tales. There are references to their schools, where they taught their pupils the lore of druidry. The training was evidently oral, the teaching was done by question and answer, and by the master intoning the information while the class repeated it in chorus. This, at any rate, is the inference from the fact that the Old Irish verb for 'teach', *for-cain*, means literally 'to sing over'. In the tales the druids function as prophets and sooth-sayers, and take and interpret omens from the cries or flight of birds and the like. They believed notably that certain days were lucky for starting under-takings, and others unlucky. For instance the boy Cú Chulainn overhears Cathbad, the chief druid, teaching his school, and one of the hundred pupils asks what that day was lucky for. Cathbad replies that anyone who took arms that day would be famous in Ireland for ever. Cú Chulainn hurries off to the king and demands to take arms, not waiting to hear the rest.[1] So too when Queen Medb is about to set out with the army on the great cattle raid the prophets and druids will not let her start for a fortnight while they wait for a favourable omen, and when they do start her charioteer suggests that they may avert the ill-luck which she fears by turning the chariot sun-wise, in the traditionally lucky direction. The word for 'prophet' is *fáith*, which is the exact Celtic cognate of the Latin *vatis*.

In addition to these two classes of the learned there was a third, the poets and literary men. In original Celtic the poets had been called generically *bardi*, 'bards', but in early Ireland the word seems to have become depressed in status by the differentiation of a specially highly trained class of poets and sages called *filid*, which means etymologically 'seers'. These appear to have usurped some of the functions of the druids and prophets, but possibly not until the Christian period when those pagan officials naturally vanished away. From early sources other than the hero tales we learn that the *filid* and *baird* were likewise trained in schools,

[1] *TBC* I, ll. 546 ff.

24

where they were taught by a qualified *fili*. The course lasted from seven to twelve years; and they learned composition in the various metres, antiquarian and other tradition (no doubt including genealogy), a very large number of the classic tales, and in their last year spells and magic. Their songs were recited to the music of the harp. The 'bardic schools' remained alive in Ireland until the vanishing of the traditional Gaelic way of life and the Gaelic aristocracy which supported them, in the seventeenth century, but there is an account of them extant, referring to this period, which shows still the long training and something of its character. The teacher taught metres and set subjects for composition, which was done by the pupils in their heads, lying on their beds in the dark; and then they recited their verses to him for correction.[1] The method of composition in Gaelic Scotland was very much the same, according to a description dating from the end of the seventeenth century. The poet shut himself indoors for a whole day, and lay on his bed in the dark, with his head covered with his plaid, while

[1] See the account in the Memoirs of the Marquis of Clanrickarde (Dublin, 1722; referring to the seventeenth century); on which see Bergin, *The Ivernian Journal*, v, no. 19 (April–June 1913). For the reference to Gaelic Scotland, see Martin Martin, *A Description of the Western Islands of Scotland* (written *c.* 1695; 1st ed., London, 1703; 4th ed., by D. J. Macleod, Stirling, 1934: see pp. 176 f.). For other accounts of the bards in the seventeenth century, see Maidment, *Analecta Scotica*, i, 118, 121, 124.

he composed a panegyric. This tradition of oral composition, not written, is very remarkable at this late date. Incidentally I might mention here, as a pure *obiter dictum*, that though the Irish poets were able to recite orally an immense amount of verse, including narrative verse,[1] they did *not* do so by improvisation. This is a fact which ought to be considered in relation to the current view on the composition and recitation of epic poetry.

The Celtic poet and sage was a functionary in society, and was an essential part of the aristocratic structure of that society. His prime duty was to praise and celebrate his chief and his chief's family in panegyric verse (which was traditionally what 'poetry' meant above all to the Celt), to preserve and recite his genealogy, and in all other such ways to further his fame; hence the necessity for his existence as a court official. He was free to travel and eulogise other lords, and for all such praises, whether of his own patron or another, he expected a due reward—a sword or horse or richly jewelled brooch or the like. In fact the early Laws gave him a legal right to this, and they also laid down the size of the retinue with which he might travel and which he might impose on the hospitality of his host— twenty-four men, in the case of the highest class of poet, the *ollam*. This man's rank was very high in law, equal to that of a petty king, but the poets were

---

[1] The Fenian ballads.

all protected by an unwritten but nevertheless mighty sanction, the fear of satire. In a heroic aristocracy as described, glory and good reputation were essentially necessary, and the satires of the poets were dreaded because they could sing a man's dispraises all through Ireland and destroy his fame and standing. Many passages show the importance of this, and the fear of the satire of poets is still alive in rural Ireland at the present day. As regards the function of the *fili* as a prophet, this is often illustrated in the hero tales. So, immediately after Medb has set off for Cooley, she meets a female[1] *fili* or *fáith* who has just returned to Ireland after studying the craft of the *fili* in Britain. She asks the woman to 'look' and to prophesy for her what will happen to the Connaught army. The woman duly 'looks', and reports that she sees red; that is to say, she consults her second sight and sees the army stained with blood, just as the second-sighted Theoclymenos in the Odyssey 'sees' the blood-splashed walls of Odysseus's hall before ever the slaughter of the wooers has begun.[2] Such horrible omens are a familiar motif in the hero tales, and are sometimes associated with the involuntary violation of the taboos called *geasa* which affected some of the heroes, the breaking of which was a sure foreboding of death.

[1] This must have been wholly exceptional, and very likely the story originally made her a mere spae-wife.

[2] *Odyssey*, xx, 350.

The Ulster cycle tells us very little about the religious beliefs of the people, which is perhaps natural considering the character of the material. At any rate it is clear that they were not Christians. Apart from the various non-Christian beliefs and practices already mentioned, and the occasional appearance of characters who are certainly pagan Celtic gods or supernatural beings, as well as the total absence of any reference to Christianity, there is one feature which settles the matter. The heroes' favourite oaths are 'I swear by the gods my tribe swears by', and 'I swear by the gods I worship'; and these formulae, however traditional, unquestionably belong to a heathen context, and incidentally to one in which each tribe had gods of its own. The people of the Ulster cycle may therefore be regarded without any doubt as pagans, and the stories as having grown up in a pagan society.

This whole picture of the ancient Irish heroic way of life as it is seen in the oldest tales is self-consistent, of a very marked individuality, and highly circumstantial. One can hardly doubt that it represents a genuine tradition of a society that once existed. This impression is strikingly reinforced when we examine the accounts of life among the continental Gauls and the Britons before they were overwhelmed by Rome, given by Greek and Roman authors, as well as what can be learned of their material culture from the evidence of archaeology. Various classical historians and others make comments on the habits of the Celts, Galatae, or Gauls, notably of course Caesar, Diodorus Siculus, Strabo, and Athenaeus. It is believed that these four derived most of their information from the work of Poseidonius of Apamaea,[1] who in Book 23 of his History, written about 80 B.C. but now lost, gave a sketch of the manners and customs of the Gauls in his own day; he had travelled among them himself. Even Caesar relied heavily on Poseidonius.

All sources agree on the aristocratic character of this Celtic society, and Caesar describes the common people as virtually slaves, who can take no independent political action and whose views are never consulted.[2] He says of the nobles, whom he calls the *equites*, that 'the greater their rank and resources the more vassals and clients they have about them',[3] and that the chiefs do not allow their own followers to be oppressed or cheated, since otherwise they would lose all their influence over them, the institution having been set up in early times to prevent the common people being helpless against the powerful.[4] He tells how a Helvetian nobleman called Orgetorix, who was to be tried for a plot against the state, brought with him to court a large number of retainers and all his clients and debtors,

[1] On the debt of these authors to Poseidonius, see *CEP*, pp. 189 ff.

[2] *BG*, VI, 13.   [3] *BG*, VI, 15.   [4] *BG*, VI, 11.

and so overawed his enemies.[1] Athenaeus quotes Poseidonius as saying that the Celts have companions whom they call 'hangers-on'.[2] All this might well have been said of the early Irish *céili*, and very likely the word Poseidonius rendered as 'hangers-on' was the Gaulish cognate or equivalent of that very term, since it means 'fellow, companion'.

The fierceness and boastfulness of the Celts is emphasised by Diodorus,[3] who describes their terrifying appearance and their fondness for exaggeration; and tells how they glorify themselves and try to depreciate others by boasting and threatening and dramatising themselves. Strabo too says they are mad on war, high-spirited and prompt to fight,[4] and foolishly boastful.[5] These features are seen also in the custom, mentioned by Diodorus,[6] by which a champion would come forward when two opposing armies were drawn up and challenge the bravest of the other army to a duel; and, when one accepted, he says, 'they sing the praises of their ancestors' brave deeds and declare their own courageous virtues, abusing and crying down their opponent and in general depriving him of his boldness of spirit by their words'. The custom of duelling before the armies is of course illustrated in

[1] *BG*, I, 4.
[2] Athenaeus, VI, 49. The word is παράσιτος.
[3] Diodorus, V, 31.   [4] Strabo, IV, iv, 2.
[5] Strabo, IV, iv, 5.   [6] Diodorus, V, 29.

the famous story of Manlius Torquatus. When a Gaulish army was threatening Rome in 360 B.C. a gigantic warrior came out in front and challenged to single combat any Roman who would accept. Manlius took up the challenge, killed the Gaul, took his typical Gaulish golden torque or collar, and was hence nicknamed Torquatus.[1] All this reminds one of the duels between Cú Chulainn and the champions picked from the Connaught army in the Cattle Raid of Cooley, and of the boastful way in which the Irish warriors tried to make good their claim to the Champion's Portion by putting their opponents to shame. I mentioned earlier how Conchobar's men swore to stand their ground though the earth split under them and the sky on top of them. This seems to have been a proverbial expression among the Celts and known as such to the Greeks, for Ptolemy son of Lagos, one of Alexander the Great's officers, told a story which is mentioned by Strabo[2] and Arrian[3] that when the Celts living on the Adriatic sent envoys to Alexander he asked them what it was they feared most—the expected answer being of course 'Alexander'—; but the mutton-headed Celts did not understand diplomacy, and could only say they feared nothing, unless perhaps that the heavens might fall on them. Similarly Aristotle says[4] that the typical rash man

[1] Livy, VII, 10.   [2] Strabo, VII, iii, 8.
[3] *Anabasis*, I, iv, 6.   [4] *Nicomachean Ethics*, III, vii, 7.

fears neither earthquakes nor waves, 'as they say of the Celts'.

Several sources speak of the clothing of the Gauls; of the striped or checked woollen cloaks fastened with brooches and the tunics of various colours, woven with gold, just like the early Irish dress; also trousers, gold collars or torques, armlets, bracelets, and rings.[1] Diodorus describes[2] the long swords, spears with long and broad iron heads, and javelins. Some of these spears he speaks of as 'like a screw', so that they not only cut but also mangled the flesh, and when they were pulled out the wound was torn open. This reminds one curiously of the *gae bulga*, though it would be rash to assert that there is any connection. One must envisage this Gaulish spear as having some kind of wavy blade like a Malayan *kris*, perhaps with barbs; such spears, belonging to the La Tène period—the so-called 'flame' spear-head—have actually been found in Gaul. Strabo mentions the long sword, spears, and javelin, and also the sling.[3] The long iron slashing sword is of course characteristic of the La Tène culture everywhere, including Ireland, and suits the descriptions in the hero tales. The sling, too, is familiar in archaeological contexts of the period as it is in the Ulster tales. Great quantities of sling-stones were found in the excavations at Maiden Castle in Dorset,

[1] E.g. Diodorus, v, 27 and 30; Strabo, iv, iv, 3 and 5.
[2] Diodorus, v, 30. [3] Strabo, iv, iv, 3.

a La Tène fortress of the first century B.C., and one of the purposes of its enormously wide ramparts is believed to have been to keep the attackers beyond sling range until their rush had been broken by the embankments, and they could be picked off by the slings of the defenders as they climbed them. The total absence of the bow and arrow in the early Irish stories is paralleled by the virtually complete lack of archaeological evidence for them in the pre-Roman period in Gaul and the British Isles; one may say that the Celts of the Iron Age made almost no use of the bow.

Greek and Roman authors agree, too, on the war-chariot as the classic feature of Celtic tactics, though it had gone out of use on the continent a generation before Caesar's time. Diodorus mentions[1] the two-horse chariot with the warrior and his charioteer, and tells how they charge, the warrior hurling his spears and then dismounting and fighting on foot with his sword. They bring their freemen with them, he says, as charioteers. Livy speaks[2] of the Gaulish chariots at the battle of Sentinum in 295 B.C. When Caesar landed in Britain in 55 B.C. his men were thrown into confusion by an attack of cavalry and chariots as they tried to disembark,[3] and next year a similar force set on his army some distance from their landing point. The assaults were continued, and

[1] Diodorus, V, 29.   [2] Livy, X, 28.
[3] BG, IV, 24.

33

the Britons tried to draw the Roman cavalry off in pursuit of the chariots, and then jumped out and attacked on foot. The British king Cassivellaunus was roughly handled by Caesar, and having given up hope of victory in a pitched battle he decided on guerilla war. He sent away most of his troops, but nevertheless still kept with him the immense number of about four thousand chariots to harass the Roman army.[1] This gives some idea of the very large part that chariots played in British warfare in the first century B.C. Caesar actually gives a description of their tactics,[2] saying that they were accustomed to drive about all over the battle-field hurling spears, and throwing the Roman ranks into confusion; and then, having penetrated the cavalry, they leaped out to fight on foot while their charioteers took the chariots to wait just outside the battle, ready to rescue them if they were routed. He speaks of their skill in managing the horses, and how the warriors climbed out on to the chariot-pole and even on to the yoke, presumably in the effort to get nearer the enemy. The Caledonians used chariots against Agricola in Scotland in the battle of Mons Graupius in A.D. 84,[3] and the last time we hear of chariots in Britain is as late as the early part of the third century, when Dio Cassius[4] tells how the

[1] For the preceding see *BG*, V, 9 ff.
[2] *BG*, IV, 33.   [3] Tacitus, *Agricola*, 35–6.
[4] Dio Cassius, LXXVI, 12.

Pictish tribes of Caledonians and Meatae went to war in chariots drawn by small, fast horses.

The two-wheeled war-chariot of the La Tène Celts is one of the most remarkable archaeological features of their culture, going back to the fifth century B.C. Examples of actual chariots have been found in graves in Gaul, particularly in the Marne region and round the middle Rhine. They are small and light, with twelve-spoked wooden wheels having iron nave-bands and iron tyres shrunk on to the felloes by a process which is probably a Celtic invention. The wheel-base was four feet six inches, and the platform four feet square. They were drawn by two ponies yoked to a pole, and having harness decorated with elaborate and beautiful enamelled bronze trappings. It is known that in the third or second century B.C. an invasion of a Gaulish warrior aristocracy settled in eastern Yorkshire and brought the Gaulish war-chariot with it; and actual specimens of this have been found in burials in the East Riding, exactly as they have in France.[1] The similarity of all this to what we know of the early Irish chariots and their use is extremely striking.

Classical writers, and not only those who drew on Poseidonius, were much impressed by the peculiar

[1] It is of interest to note that some of the Yorkshire graves contained joints of pork among the grave goods; the Celtic chief was to take with him on his journey the favourite food of the Celt.

Gaulish custom of head-hunting and preserving the heads as trophies.[1] Polybius already remarks[2] on the way in which in 218 B.C. a Celtic contingent in the Roman army deserted the Romans and joined Hannibal, cutting off the heads of the Romans they killed in the mutiny. Livy too describes[3] how the Senonian Gauls defeated a legion at Clusium in 295 B.C. and rode off in triumph with the Roman heads hanging round their horses' necks or spiked on spears. Again, he tells[4] of the disastrous defeat of the Romans under Lucius Postumius by the Boii in northern Italy in 216 B.C., and how they carried off his head; and, 'as their custom is', removed the flesh, inlaid the skull with gold, and used it as a sacred vessel for libations and as a drinking-cup for their priests. But it is the authors deriving from Poseidonius who most strikingly emphasize the coincidence with ancient Ireland. Diodorus[5] and Strabo[6] tell us that the Gauls cut off the heads of those killed in battle and hung them round their

[1] The Chadwicks point out (*GL*, pp. 92 ff.) that carrying off the head of a slain enemy was also practised by the northern Germanic peoples (and one might add, by many others); but, as they remark, there is really nothing to suggest that special refinements known among the Celts were familiar to them, apart from the story of Cunimund's skull used as a drinking-cup in Paul the Deacon, and the preservation of Grettir's head in the Grettis Saga; nor even that head-hunting was a *regular* thing with them, as it was with the Gauls and Irish.

[2] Polybius, III, 67.   [3] Livy, x, 26.
[4] Livy, XXIII, 24.   [5] Diodorus, v, 29.
[6] Strabo, IV, iv, 5.

horses' necks (evidently as they rode away, just as in Livy), and then embalmed those of the most famous men among them and kept them carefully in a chest, showing them off to visitors and refusing large sums of money offered for them.[1] Strabo adds that Poseidonius says he saw this himself and was sickened by the sight at first, but afterwards became hardened to it.[2] Various archaeological discoveries have confirmed that the Gauls were in the habit of fixing skulls up on buildings to display them.[3]

The early Irish feast and the customs associated with it likewise reappear most astonishingly in the work of Poseidonius. Diodorus mentions the greed of the Gauls for imported wine,[4] and the blazing fires with cauldrons and spits loaded with great joints of meat.[5] Strabo too speaks of their great

[1] Probably offered by the relatives, to redeem them, rather than by early Celtic head-fanciers.

[2] Strabo says the Gauls nailed up the heads at the doors of their houses, but the corresponding passage in Diodorus seems to suggest that he had misunderstood Poseidonius, and that what the latter had really described as 'nailed up' was the 'blood-stained spoils', i.e. clothing, etc.

[3] At the Gaulish oppidum of Entremont, prior to the Roman conquest in 125 B.C., pillars were decorated with carved stone heads in imitation of real ones, and a lintel was found with niches for heads; also skulls with nails through them, which had obviously been nailed up. See *Gallia*, XII (1954), 285 ff. Similar finds were made at Roquepertuse and elsewhere; *Revue des Études Anciennes*, LVIII (1956), 272. See A. Grenier, *Les Gaulois* (Paris, 1945), 203 f.

[4] Diodorus, V, 26.

[5] Diodorus, V, 28.

eating,[1] with milk and all kinds of meat, pork above all, and Athenaeus tells[2] that their food is a few loaves and a great amount of meat, boiled or roast, which they eat like wild beasts by taking up whole joints in both hands and gnawing off the flesh. At a feast the chief man present sits in the middle, with the host next to him and the rest ranged on either side in order of precedence, guarded by their shieldbearers, and servants carry round wine in fluted jars and meat on platters. Diodorus says,[3] 'They honour brave men with the finest pieces of meat', and that at banquets they are in the habit of getting into disputes and challenging each other to mortal duels. Athenaeus, explicitly quoting Poseidonius, also speaks of the duels at feasts,[4] adding, 'Formerly when the hindquarters were served up the bravest took the thigh-bone, and if anyone challenged this the two arose and fought a duel to the death'. This reads exactly like a description of the Irish custom of the Champion's Portion and the resulting fights; and the words which I have already quoted in a different context about the Gaulish practice of boasting and seeking to deprive one's opponent of his courage, illustrate just what happened in the Irish hall. That there is no connection between the Gaulish and the Irish in all this is more than I, for one, am prepared to believe.

[1] Strabo, IV, iv, 3.   [2] Athenaeus, IV, 36.
[3] Diodorus, V, 28.   [4] Athenaeus, IV, 40.

Concerning the druids and other classes of learned men, the authors who used Poseidonius seem to have misunderstood him, including particularly Caesar, who attributed everything to the druids and exaggerated their powers.[1] Still, he gives some valuable information on their training. He speaks of their schools, to which pupils flocked, and mentions that their discipline was thought to have been invented in Britain and brought over to Gaul, saying that whoever wanted to perfect his studies went to Britain to learn more. They memorised great quantities of verse, and some continued their training for twenty years. They refused to use writing for these purposes, though they employed Greek letters in other affairs.[2] All this is extraordinarily like what we know of the education in Ireland, not so much of the druids, about which little is known, as of the *filid*, notably the very long training and the oral character of the literary tradition; and I would stress the belief that Britain was the place for post-graduate studies, comparing the Irish passage quoted earlier about the poetess or prophetess returning from Britain after having learned the arts of poetry. It looks rather as if there may have been a tradition to that effect among the western Celts. Strabo tells us[3] there were three classes of learned men among the Gauls—the bards,

---

[1] Cf. *CEP*, pp. 210, 224.   [2] *BG*, VI, 13–14.
[3] Strabo, IV, iv, 4.

the *vates*, and the druids; the bards being poets, the *vates* interpreters of sacrifices—that is, soothsayers— and the druids philosophers—that is, priests. This corresponds so exactly to the Irish *bard*, *fáith*, and *druí*, even to the very names, that it must be genuine and must represent a real situation among the Celtic peoples. Moreover, it best suits what a study of the sources suggests Poseidonius himself originally said, as Tierney has shown.[1] Diodorus[2] speaks of the 'lyric poets called βάρδοι', who sing eulogies and satires to the accompaniment of a stringed instrument; the druids, whom he treats as philosophers and theologians; and the seers, who foretell the future by sacrificing animals and humans. For 'seers' he uses the Greek μάντεις, not a Celtic word. The Celtic triumvirate of **bardos*, **vātis*, and **druvids* is confirmed by Ammianus Marcellinus,[3] who probably derives from Poseidonius via Timagenes. He calls the three *bardi*, *euhages*, and *dryides*, but the unknown word *euhages* is probably a mere scribal corruption of Poseidonius's οὐάτεις.[4] The functions of the Gaulish bard are well illustrated in a story told by Poseidonius and best recorded by Athenaeus,[5] which could just as well have been told of Ireland at any period as long as the tradition of the court poets lasted. A Gaulish

[1] *CEP*, pp. 210, 224.   [2] Diodorus, v, 31.
[3] Ammianus, xv, ix, 8.   [4] Cf. *CEP*, p. 210.
[5] Athenaeus, IV, 37.

40

chief called Lovernius, 'Fox', drove in his chariot scattering gold and silver to those who followed on foot, and gave a great free banquet for many days to all who wished to take part. At last the feast ended, but a certain poet who had arrived too late came to Lovernius with an ode in which he glorified Lovernius's greatness and lamented that he himself was too late for the feast. Lovernius, delighted with the poem, called for a bag of gold and threw it to him as he ran beside the chariot. Picking it up, the bard composed another song to him, in which he said that the very tracks of his chariot in the earth gave gold and benefits to mankind. One can almost hear this ode in the Irish bardic style and language.

As to the Celtic gods and religious beliefs, the subject is too large to handle here. It must be enough to mention that a number of the characters in Irish legends who are evidently gods bear the same names, and have some of the same attributes, as Gaulish or British gods known from Roman or Romano-Celtic sources. No classical author mentions any equivalent of the strange Irish *geis* or taboo, but the Irish practice of divination and the belief in lucky and unlucky days are well known on the Continent. The celebrated Calendar of Coligny, a fragmentary Gaulish calendar of the first–second centuries A.D., on bronze plates, gives all the months of the year, with their Gaulish names, and all the days with peg-holes for the insertion of a peg to mark the day; and some of the days are labelled *matis*, 'lucky', and others *anmatis*, 'unlucky'. The custom of moving sun-wise, and regarding it as unlucky to do otherwise and to go 'widdershins', is paralleled in Gaul by Athenaeus's remark[1] that they do reverence to the gods by turning to the right, and that the servants pouring out wine do so in the same direction, that is, to the guest's left.

We have here, then, a number of passages in Greek and Roman historians describing the way of life of the Gauls, and to some extent of the Britons, in the Early Iron Age, before that way of life was extinguished by the heavy weight of the civilisation of Rome; and we have also the considerable corroboration on the material side derived from archaeology. The whole constitutes a picture which agrees rather remarkably, I think we must all feel, with that which we find in the early Irish traditional tales illustrating the nature of life in ancient Ireland. How far is it legitimate to make this comparison, and to take the further step, as has often been done before and as I shall today, of suggesting that there is a significant connection? Clearly, not all the parallels quoted are individually at all decisive; for instance, many barbarian peoples have worn cloaks and tunics, or have believed in lucky and unlucky days, or have enjoyed eating pork. But some of the others are more significant and a good deal more

[1] Athenaeus, IV, 36.

weighty. Among these we may reckon the rather peculiar system of clientship;[1] the close likeness in the construction and tactics of the two-horse, two-wheeled war chariot with its iron tyres and the rest; the practice of head-hunting and the very special customs of preserving heads as trophies associated with it; the quite extraordinary ceremony of the Champion's Portion and the fights to which it led; and the threefold institution of bard, prophet, and druid, *bardos*, *vātis*, and *druvids*. Perhaps one may even include, as a slight but significant parallel, the proverbial joke about fearing nothing except that the earth may split under a man and the sky fall on him. Other similarities I have mentioned, while not in themselves at all so conclusive, do help to corroborate, and to emphasise the general agreement between the habits of the Gauls and Britons in the first century B.C. and those of the early Irish at a date which I have not yet clearly indicated and which must be considered next. Whatever the date, and however improbable some of us may instinctively feel this to be, I think we must conclude that there is a connection of some sort between the two.

The medieval Irish antiquarian historians had no doubts about the date. They fitted the Ulster cycle into their elaborately constructed scheme of Irish

[1] It is not at all the same as the *comitatus*, the picked professional band of guards, characteristic of the early Germanic peoples.

43

history by placing the events about the time of the birth of Christ, and this date is rather generally and quite uncritically accepted. But we must ask ourselves what independent evidence the antiquarians had for this, and when we do so we find the answer is that they had none. It is impossible to push back the beginning of what may fairly be called the *historical* period in Ireland earlier than the fifth century, or in certain respects the fourth, if we treat history conscientiously and use only those documents which may reasonably be called 'historical'. Of course, if we are prepared to accept late copies of traditional sagas of unknown date and of obvious legendary character as history, then we can put Irish 'history' almost as far back as we choose; and this has in fact far too often been done.[1] But any honest

[1] I should emphasise that what I mean here is the historicity of persons and events; for instance, Conn and Eóghan, kings of the north and south of Ireland respectively, reputed by the sages to have lived in the second century, are quite obviously legendary and indeed mythological characters, and the events in which they are said to have taken part are clearly bogus (see my *Cath Maighe Léna*, Mediaeval and Modern Irish Series, vol. IX, Dublin 1938, pp. xxiv ff.). The same is true of still later characters like Cormac mac Airt. It is probably not too much to say that the earliest figure whom we can regard with any confidence as at all historical is Niall of the Nine Hostages. Equally, then, the characters Conchobar and Cú Chulainn, Ailill and Medb and the rest, and the events of the Cattle Raid of Cooley, are themselves entirely legend and purely un-historical. But this does *not* mean that the traditional background, the setting, in which the Ulster cycle was built up is bogus; the whole of this lecture is intended to show that it is not. In the same way, Agamemnon

historian must admit that this is simply to beg the question. The Irish antiquarians themselves had no means of dating the Ulster cycle, or any other body of story or tradition before the fourth to fifth centuries. Their only independent native source for the period before the fifth century which may fairly be regarded as a secondary historical one is the traditional, orally preserved genealogies of the royal and princely families of Ireland. Now, it was part of the activity of the medieval antiquarians that they set about carrying these back, far beyond the stage where they began to be genuine, by the simple process of adding bogus names at the beginning; particularly with the chief royal families, which were derived in this easy way from no less an ancestor than Adam. A careful examination of the pedigrees shows that some of them are evidently and some others probably genuine as far back as the fifth century and even the fourth, but that these mostly converge about this time on one or two lines whose earlier generations are the names of fanciful characters, divinities, and so on, with clear traces of a belief in descent from the gods; on which is super-imposed a thick layer of biblical and antiquarian

and Helen are doubtless not historical, and an Achilles never killed a Hector nor a Priam ransomed the body; but the Mycenaean world dimly depicted in Homer was a real one, and there may well have been hostilities between it and N.W. Asia Minor —just as there may well have been between pre-historic Ulster and the rest of Ireland.

ecclesiastical learning. This converging means that the sages had no genuine tradition beyond that point, and so tied a given genealogy on to a greater one for which they thought they had such a tradition. Moreover, none of them link up at all clearly or convincingly with any of the characters of the Ulster cycle, and very few make even any pretence to do so. The main factor which was responsible for the idea that the Ulster stories belong to the time of the birth of Christ is an obviously spurious tale that king Conchobar was converted to Christianity on hearing through a druid that Jesus had just been crucified,[1] a typical medieval Irish legend springing from the wish that one's favourite ancient pagan heroes should not languish in Hell but should miraculously have become Christians. The consequence of all this is that independent Irish tradition can give us no guidance as to the date of the formation of the Ulster cycle of stories, and that we must rely on the internal evidence alone.

This is a good deal more helpful. At the time when Irish history proper begins, say in the fifth century, the political framework of Ireland was constituted by seven separate kingdoms—Munster, Leinster, Connaught, Meath, Ailech, Oriel, and Ulster, the last being at this stage merely a small part of North-east Ireland, roughly the modern

[1] See K. Meyer, *Death Tales of the Ulster Heroes* (Royal Irish Academy Todd Lecture Series, XIV, 1906), pp. 4 ff.

counties of Antrim and Down. The southern half of Ireland was ruled by a dynasty of overlords called the Eóghanacht; and the whole northern half except the small Ulster just mentioned was in the hands of a group of families who traced their descent to Niall of the Nine Hostages, who is supposed to have died in the year 404. Two of these northern dynasties shared between them the 'High Kingship', that is to say they claimed an overlordship over Ireland as a whole. But there are clear signs that this whole political structure was quite new in the fifth century, and that it was not yet fully established in Niall's time. The kingdoms which now made up between them most of what we think of as the greater Ulster, that is Ailech chiefly in Donegal, and Oriel in most of the rest of the north between this and Lough Neagh, were new creations, probably dating from the fifth century itself.[1] The older, powerful Ulster of the hero tales was smashed into fragments by the family of Niall. Now, in the hero tales themselves there is no trace of any of this. There, Ireland consists of a great Ulster on the one hand, and the rest of the country, under the hegemony of Connaught, on the other. There is no sign of Ailech or Oriel, or of a High Kingship, or of the southern dynasty of the Eóghanacht, and there are only five great kingdoms, not seven. Ulster is ruled from Emain Macha; which is not even within the

[1] See Binchy in *Studia Hibernica*, II, 150 ff.

new, small 'Ulster' of the early historical period, but in Oriel. It is obvious that the Ulster of the hero tales represents that kingdom before it was broken to pieces in the fifth century, and that these tales show us a polity of Ireland which is 'pre-historic' in exactly the same sense as the Mycenaean polity preserved in the *Iliad* is 'pre-historic'. This gives a most valuable starting-point—the Ulster cycle represents a state of affairs older than the fifth century. This date is remarkably confirmed by other factors. I have already pointed out that the people of the Ulster cycle were pagans and that it contains no traces of Christianity. But Ireland was converted in the course of the fifth century, and once again therefore internal evidence shows that the background of the tales belongs to a period before that time. Then, too, the characteristic use of the war-chariot is itself 'pre-historic', since there is no reliable evidence whatever for its existence in Irish warfare in historical times; one or two instances which have been claimed really belong to sources which have undergone the influence of the heroic tradition.[1]

If the formation of the tradition is older, then, than the fifth century, how much older is it? An attempt was made by Ridgeway to answer this question, just short of sixty years ago, in his lecture 'The Date of the First Shaping of the Cuchulainn

[1] The examples claimed by Ridgeway, in *PBA*, II, 7 f., are all valueless, for various reasons.

Saga'.[1] Ridgeway accepted unquestioningly the Irish tradition that the tales belong to the time of the birth of Christ, and tried to corroborate this with archaeological evidence. He made a study of the material objects mentioned in the stories, and had no difficulty in showing the presence of La Tène elements among them; though unfortunately a good many of his points are of no value at all, either because the precise meanings of the names for the objects are unknown, or because they were unknown to Ridgeway,[2] or because the passages in which they occur are late interpolations, or for other reasons, so that the result is largely inconclusive. For instance he tried to demonstrate the presence in the *Táin* of La Tène helmets, but the only place where helmets are clearly mentioned is an interpolation of the eleventh century. Ridgeway had the right idea, but unfortunately he spoiled it all by a slip in his reasoning. He argued that the La Tène culture died out in Gaul by the beginning of the Christian era, and in Britain by the end of the first century, and that in Ireland it can therefore hardly have lasted beyond about A.D. 150, and *therefore* that the traditional date for the Ulster cycle is about right. He had neglected to consider that the reason why it died out in Gaul and Britain at

[1] *PBA*, II.
[2] His real knowledge of the Cattle Raid of Cooley may be gauged by the fact that he refers to it as 'these poems'.

these dates is that it was overwhelmed there by the quite different civilisation of Rome; and that as this never came to Ireland there is no cause whatever to put the end of the Irish La Tène era at any such early period. In fact we know that it lingered on until the arrival of the new cultural influences which reached Ireland with the coming of Christianity, and that some of its art-motifs were even adopted into the new art style, as I have already remarked. Consequently this line of reasoning gives us no date older than the one already arrived at, that is, 'before the fifth century'.

Before attempting a final solution it would be as well to look at the question of the *terminus post quem*. The extraordinary similarities between life in the Ulster cycle and life among the Gauls and Britons in the second and first centuries B.C., with their La Tène Iron Age civilisation, have already been stressed; and we have also seen that a Gaulish chariot-using aristocracy had established itself in Yorkshire perhaps as early as the third century B.C. The history of the way in which the La Tène culture reached Ireland is still not by any means clear, but recent opinion suggests that it was by two routes. One immigration, a somewhat earlier one, probably came to southern and central Ireland direct from Gaul, and the other, rather later, from Gaul via northern Britain into Ulster and to some extent to the south of that. The northern influx seems in fact to have had cultural affinities with the Yorkshire La Tène colony just mentioned. It may in part represent an offshoot of these people who reached northern Ireland in the second century B.C. or earlier and retained their identity for some centuries;[1] and would mean that the colonists brought with them various features such as their characteristic swords and sword-scabbards (some with continental affinities of the third century B.C.),[2] their harness-trappings and so on, with typical La Tène decoration, and notably the use of the La Tène war-chariot. If so, and considering everything that has been said today, the idea that the picture of life in Ireland, and notably Ulster, in the 'heroic age' found in the Ulster tales is in effect a picture of life among the descendants of these La Tène Celts of northern British and ultimately of Gaulish origin surely does not seem an unreasonable or even a rash one. It would not follow, of course, that the tradition of epic prose story-telling, and with it the background of the Ulster hero tales, is in a strict sense anything like so old as the period when these

[1] For an important account of recent archaeological opinion, and for some very clear and original thought on the subject, see E. Rynne, 'The Introduction of La Tène into Ireland', in *Bericht über den V. Internationalen Kongress für Vor- und Frühgeschichte, Hamburg* (Union Internationale des Sciences Préhistoriques et Protohistoriques); Berlin, 1961; pp. 705 ff.

[2] See M. Jope in S. Frere (ed.), *Problems of the Iron Age in Southern Britain* (1961), pp. 79 ff.

immigrants reached Ulster; but the date of their arrival does give a *terminus post quem*, and if we accept the premisses it follows that the formation of the tradition falls somewhere in the period between the second century B.C. and the fourth century A.D.

These are very wide limits, and it is surely possible to reduce them, by the consideration of a point which has not yet been raised and must now be faced. The oldest manuscript containing tales of the Ulster cycle, the Book of the Brown Cow, was written by a monk at Clonmacnoise about the year 1100. It is generally agreed that the so-called Version I of the Cattle Raid of Cooley contained in this manuscript was compiled in the eleventh century by conflating two distinct written versions of the ninth century now lost, the discrepancies between them being due to oral differentiation. However, the story with all its present essential episodes is known to have existed already in the first half of the eighth century,[1] and it is believed that it may have been recorded in writing as early as the middle of the seventh.[2] It is unlikely that there was any written text earlier than that, since the use of writing as we know it did not reach Ireland before the fifth century and was almost certainly not applied to the

[1] For a discussion and demonstration of these points see R. Thurneysen, *Die Irische Helden- und Königsage* (Halle, 1921), pp. 99 ff.

[2] For this revision of opinion see Thurneysen, *ZCP*, XIX, 193 ff.

native literature before the end of the sixth at the earliest. In that case, granted that the stories had been handed on previously by oral tradition, and that the picture of the background against which it was felt such stories should be composed had been formulated not later than the fourth century as already suggested, the further we try to push this formulation back before that time the less convincing the claim becomes. To declare with confidence that it belongs to a period about the time of the birth of Christ, but that the stories were not written down till some 650 years later, stretches one's credulity rather far. Is it credible that a story-telling tradition could be handed on orally without very great change over such a vast period of time? Many people would think that it is not, and would scout any such idea. We must remember, however, that the early Irish *filid* and story-tellers were professionals who had had a rigorous training, part of which was aimed at perfecting them in this very thing, at memorising and reciting and handing on a large number of traditional tales. It was their business, and they were highly skilled at it. In such circumstances stories may be passed on for centuries without any really fundamental change. I do not think, therefore, that it is at all extravagant to claim that a body of narrative first written down in the seventh century may have been formulated in, say, the fourth or possibly even earlier and handed on orally for 300 years or so by the professional Irish reciters in the way described. After all, in the early Germanic epic cycle we find not merely a description of the background of the Germanic tribes in the migration period of the fourth to fifth centuries but even references to known historical people of that date and poetic accounts of events which had a historical reality; and yet the earliest epics telling of these things are not older than the seventh century at the earliest. For that matter, the *Iliad* is believed to preserve a record of something that happened in the twelfth century B.C., and to contain in it descriptions of ancient Greek life some centuries older, and yet it must have been handed down orally and not written until the eighth century. Considering everything, then, it does seem quite legitimate to claim an oral life of some 300 years or thereabouts for the Irish epic tales, but in proportion as we try to put them further back we increase the burden of proof on ourselves; and to try to date them about the time of the birth of Christ is asking too much, and asking it quite unnecessarily. The La Tène civilisation introduced to Ireland well before that time must have continued to exist without any cultural break, untouched by the Roman Empire or the Anglo-Saxons alike, until the fifth century brought changes which altered the quality of Irish life and the character of Irish art; so that the Ulster tales might perfectly well have been put together more or less as we have them in, say, the fourth century A.D. and not earlier. That there is nothing whatsoever in the traditional 'about the time of the birth of Christ' has already been shown.

This being so, I think it is not unfair to say that though we cannot claim that any of the persons or events are historical, the extremely circumstantial account of the life and civilisation depicted in the Ulster tales is demonstrably older than the fifth century and extraordinarily similar to that of the Gauls and Britons in the couple of centuries before they were absorbed by Rome; and that the reason for this is that Gauls, Britons, and Irish were all living in cultures which were local expressions of a Celtic Early Iron Age whose common roots lay in Gaul in the third century B.C. In other words, if we want to know what it was to be a late La Tène Celt, and what life in the Early Iron Age was like, we can get some notion of it by reading the Irish Ulster cycle of hero stories. Hence, I submit, the title of this lecture is not altogether fanciful or without justification.[1]

[1] I wish to express my warmest thanks to my friend and colleague Professor Stuart Piggott for kindly letting me consult him about some matters of Iron Age archaeology, and for his helpful comments. Any errors are of course entirely my own.

This lecture was delivered by Professor K. H. Jackson
in the University of Cambridge on 14 May 1964